Book Four

Draw · Write · NOW·®

by
Marie Hablitzel
and
Kim Stitzer

*A Drawing and
Handwriting
Course for Kids!*

Barker Creek Publishing, Inc. • Poulsbo, Washington

Dedicated to...

...my grandchildren.
I have enjoyed drawing with you! — M.H.

...Tyler's teachers—Ann Healy Raymond, Shirley Parrott, Bob Good and Kathleen Moncrief — K.S.

The text on the handwriting pages is set in a custom
font created from Marie Hablitzel's handwriting.
The drawings are done using Prismacolor pencils
outlined with a black PaperMate FLAIR!® felt tip pen.
A Prismacolor Clear Blender was used to blend the colors on the cover.

Published by Barker Creek Publishing, Inc.
P.O. Box 2610 • Poulsbo, WA 98370-2610
800•692•5833 FAX: 360•613•2542
www.barkercreek.com

Text and Illustration Copyright © 1997 by Kim Hablitzel Stitzer

Book layout by Judy Richardson
Computer graphics by Gregg Scott
Printed in Hong Kong through Mandarin Offset

Library of Congress Catalog Card Number: 93-73893

Publisher's Cataloging in Publication Data:
Hablitzel, Marie, 1920 -
Draw•Write•Now®, Book Four: A drawing and handwriting course for kids!
(fourth in series)
Summary: A collection of drawing and handwriting lessons for children. **Book Four** focuses on The Polar Regions, The Arctic and The Antarctic. Fourth book in the ***Draw•Write•Now®*** series. — 1st ed.
1. Drawing—Technique—Juvenile Literature. 2. Drawing—Study and Teaching (Elementary). 3. Penmanship. 4. Arctic Region—Juvenile Literature. 5. Antarctica—Juvenile Literature. 6. Arctic Peoples—Juvenile Literature.
I. Stitzer, Kim, 1956 -   , coauthor. II. Title.
741.2   [372.6]—dc 19

ISBN: 0-9639307-4-5

First Printing

About this book...

For most children, drawing is their first form of written communication. Long before they master the alphabet and sentence syntax, children express themselves creatively on paper through line and color.

As children mature, their imaginations often race ahead of their drawing skills. By teaching them to see complex objects as combinations of simple shapes and encouraging them to develop their fine-motor skills through regular practice, they can better record the images they see so clearly in their minds.

This book contains a collection of beginning drawing lessons and text for practicing handwriting. These lessons were developed by a teacher who saw her second-grade students becoming increasingly frustrated with their drawing efforts and disenchanted with repetitive handwriting drills.

For over 30 years, Marie Hablitzel refined what eventually became a daily drawing and handwriting curriculum. Marie's premise was simple—drawing and handwriting require many of the same skills. And, regular practice in a supportive environment is the key to helping children develop their technical

Coauthors Marie Hablitzel (left) and her daughter, Kim Stitzer

skills, self-confidence and creativity. As a classroom teacher, Marie intertwined her daily drawing and handwriting lessons with math, science, social studies, geography, reading and creative writing. She wove an educational tapestry that hundreds of children have found challenging, motivating —and fun!

Although Marie is now retired, her drawing and handwriting lessons continue to be used in the classroom. With the assistance of her daughter, Kim Stitzer, Marie shares over 150 of her creative lessons in the eight-volume *Draw•Write•Now®* series.

In *Draw•Write•Now®, Book One,* children explore life on a farm, kids and critters and storybook characters. *Books Two* through *Six* feature topics as diverse as Christopher Columbus, the weather, Native Americans, the polar regions, young George Washington, beaver ponds and life in the sea. In *Draw•Write•Now®, Books Seven and Eight,* children circle the globe while learning about animals of the world.

We hope your children and students enjoy these lessons as much as ours have!

—*Carolyn Hurst, Publisher*

Look for these books in the *Draw•Write•Now®* series...

Book One: On the Farm, Kids and Critters, Storybook Characters
Book Two: Christopher Columbus, Autumn Harvest, The Weather
Book Three: Native Americans, North America, The Pilgrims
Book Four: The Polar Regions, The Arctic, The Antarctic
Book Five: The United States, Abraham Lincoln, George Washington
Book Six: On the Land, Life in Ponds and Rivers, In the Sea
Book Seven: Animals of the World, Part I
Book Eight: Animals of the World, Part II

...coming soon from Barker Creek Publishing.
For additional information call 1-800-692-5833
or visit our web site at www.barkercreek.com

Table of Contents

A table of contents is like a map. It guides you to the places you want to visit in a book. Pick a subject you want to draw, then turn to the page listed beside the picture.

For more information on the *Draw•Write•Now*® series, see page 3. For suggestions on how to use this book, see page 6.

 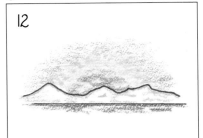
 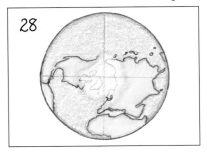

 34

 36

 38

 40

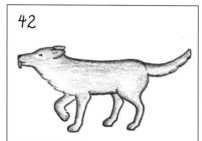 42

 44

46 Draw Your World!   48 Learn More!

The Antarctic   Page 49

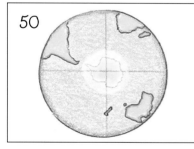 50

 52

 54

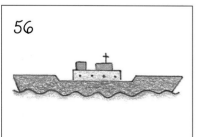 56

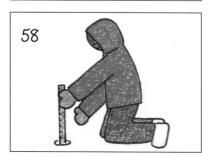 58

60 Draw From Your Imagination!   62 Learn More!

Teaching Tips   Page 63

A few tips to get started...

This is a book for children and their parents, teachers and caregivers. Although most young people can complete the lessons in this book quite successfully on their own, a little help and encouragement from a caring adult can go a long way toward building a child's self-confidence, creativity and technical skills.

Ape by Michele Fujii, age 10
from Draw•Write•Now®, Book Eight

The following outline contains insights from the 30-plus years the authors have worked with the material in this book. Realizing that no two children or classrooms are alike, the authors encourage you to modify these lessons to best suit the needs of your child or classroom. Each **Draw•Write•Now®** lesson includes five parts:

　　1. Introduce the subject.
　　2. Draw the subject.
　　3. Draw the background.
　　4. Practice handwriting.
　　5. Color the drawing.

Each child will need a pencil, an eraser, drawing paper, penmanship paper and either crayons, color pencils or felt tip markers to complete each lesson as presented here.

1. Introduce the Subject

Begin the lesson by generating interest in the subject with a story, discussion, poem, photograph or song. The questions on the illustrated notes scattered

throughout this book are examples of how interest can be built along a related theme. Answers to these questions and the titles of several theme-related books are on pages 26, 48 and 62.

2. Draw the Subject

Have the children draw with a pencil. Encourage them to draw lightly because some lines (shown as dashed lines on the drawing lessons) will need to be erased. Point out the shapes and lines in the subject as the children work through the lesson. Help the children see that complex objects can be viewed as combinations of lines and simple shapes.

Help the children be successful! Show them how to position the first step on their papers in an appropriate size. Initially, the children may find some shapes difficult to draw. If they do, provide a pattern for them to trace, or draw the first step for them. Once they fine-tune their skills and build their self-confidence, their ability and creativity will take over. For lesson-specific drawing tips and suggestions, refer to *Teaching Tips* on pages 63–64.

3. Draw the Background

Encourage the children to express their creativity and imagination in the backgrounds they add to their pictures. Add to their creative libraries by demonstrating various ways to draw trees, horizons and other details. Point out background details in the drawings in this book, illustrations from other books, photographs and works of art.

Encourage the children to draw their world by looking for basic shapes and lines in the things they see around them. Ask them to draw from their imaginations by using their developing skills. For additional ideas on motivating children to draw creatively, see pages 24–25, 46–47 and 60–61.

4. Practice Handwriting

In place of drills—rows of e's, r's and so on—it is often useful and more motivating to have children write complete sentences when practicing their handwriting. When the focus is on handwriting, rather than spelling or vocabulary enrichment, use simple words that the children can easily read and spell. Begin by writing each word with the children, demonstrating how individual letters are formed and stressing proper spacing. Start slowly. One or two sentences may be challenging enough in the beginning. Once the children are consistently forming their letters correctly, encourage them to work at their own pace.

There are many ways to adapt these lessons for use with your child or classroom. For example, you may want to replace the authors' text with your own words. You may want to let the children compose sentences to describe their drawings or answer the theme-related questions found throughout the book. You may prefer to replace the block alphabet used in this book with a cursive, D'Nealian® or other alphabet style. If you are unfamiliar with the various alphabet styles used for teaching handwriting, consult your local library. A local elementary school may also be able to recommend an appropriate alphabet style and related resource materials.

5. Color the Picture

Children enjoy coloring their own drawings. The beautiful colors, however, often cover the details they have so carefully drawn in pencil. To preserve their efforts, you may want to have the children trace their pencil lines with black crayons or fine-tipped felt markers.

Crayons—When they color with crayons, have the children outline their drawings with a black crayon *after* they have colored their pictures (the black crayon may smear if they do their outlining first).

Swan by Andrew Thorsen, age 4
from Draw•Write•Now®, Book One

Spotted Dog by Kate-Lynn Brooks, age 8
from Draw•Write•Now®, Book One

Color Pencils—When they color with color pencils, have the children outline their drawings with a felt tip marker *before* they color their drawings.

Felt Tip Markers—When they color with felt tip markers, have the children outline their drawings with a black marker *after* they have colored their pictures.

Pilgrims by Megan Forward, age 7
from Draw•Write•Now®, Book Three

Your comments are appreciated!
How are you sharing Draw•Write•Now® with your children or students? The authors would appreciate hearing from you. Write to Marie Hablitzel and Kim Stitzer, c/o Barker Creek Publishing, P.O. Box 2610, Poulsbo, WA 98370, USA.

The top and bottom of the world
are covered with ice and snow. These are the

Polar Regions

December

January

November

February

Antarctic Summer
Arctic Winter

October

March

Arctic

April

September

Antarctic

August

May

Arctic Summer
Antarctic Winter

July

June

Practice Handwriting all Year!

The more you practice, the better your handwriting will look!

The Polar Regions

The North Pole is in the Arctic.
The South Pole is in Antarctica.
They are the earth's coldest places.
Special animals live there.

Why is it so cold near the poles?

North Pole

South Pole

Question answered on page 26

Adélie Penguin

1.

2.

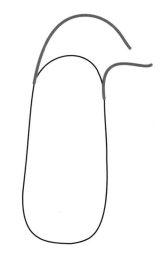

3.

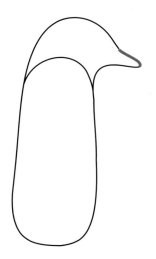

4.

5.

Adélie Penguins
live in the Antarctic.

6.

Auroras

Teaching Tip on page 64
Question answered on page 26

The Northern and Southern Lights

1.

2.

3.

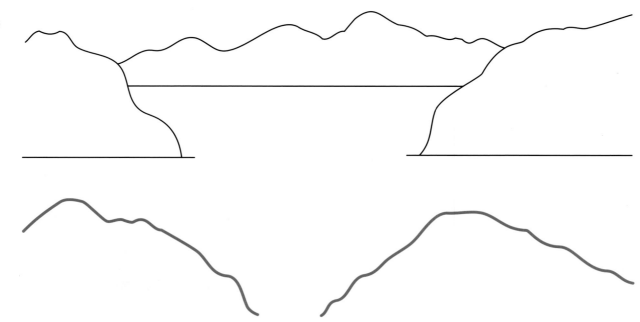

Auroras are colors in the sky.
They form around the poles.
We see them on cloudless nights.
They take different shapes.

Have you seen an aurora?

Chunks of ice float in oceans.
They are called icebergs.
Icebergs form near the poles.
They melt in warmer waters.

How do icebergs form?

Orca

1.

2.

3.

4.

Orcas are found in the Arctic and the Antarctic.

5.

6.

Ocean Migration

Question answered on page 26

Blue Whale

1.

2.

3.

4.

Blue Whales
migrate to the Arctic
and the Antarctic.

Whales live all over the world.
In summer, something happens.
Whales swim toward the poles.
We call it migration.

Why do whales migrate?

Many birds migrate.

Some fly north to the Arctic.

A few fly south to the Antarctic.

They stay all summer.

How do birds know where to go?

Arctic Loon

1.

2.

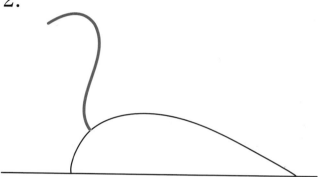

3.

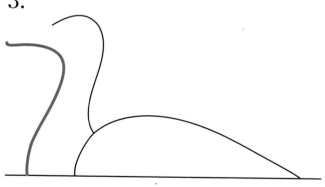

4.

5.

6.

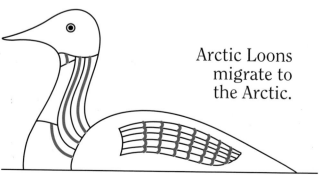

Arctic Loons
migrate to
the Arctic.

Animals that Stay

Question answered on page 26

Seal

1.

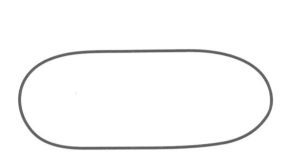

2.

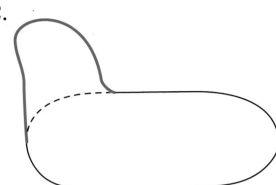

3.

4.

5.

6.

Seals live in the
Arctic and the
Antarctic.

Some animals do not migrate.
They stay in the cold all year.
Many of them have blubber.
Blubber keeps them warm.

What is blubber?

People live in the far north.
The Arctic is their home.
People visit Antarctica.
Antarctica is very cold.

Who were the
first people to
live in the
Arctic?

Question answered on page 26

Kayak

1.

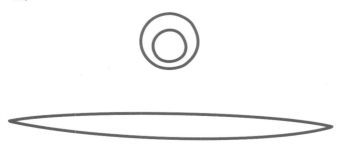

2.

3.

4.

5.

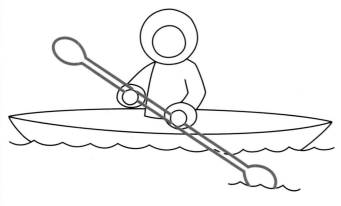

6.

Kayaks were invented by the Inuit.

Draw What You See

How can your coloring strokes add more than color to your picture?

Strokes that go
from side to side
give a calm,
smooth look.

Strokes that go
up and down
suggest
height and depth.

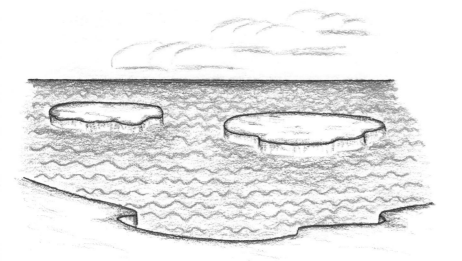

Curved strokes
suggest action.

Why are the coloring strokes...

...colored toward the wolf's tail?

...colored toward the musk ox's feet?

Auroras shift and move in the nighttime sky. How can you make your sky look active?

1. Lightly draw a line of action.

2. Cross the line of action with color (zigzag lines are active).

3. Add more colors. Overlap the edges.

4. Color the rest of the night sky. Overlap the aurora's edges.

Learn more about the polar regions...

Tilt! The earth tilts on its axis—which can be thought of as an imaginary rod that runs through the North and South Poles—blocking all sunlight to the polar regions in winter. The tilt of the earth and how it affects our world is explained in SUNSHINE MAKES THE SEASONS *by Franklyn Bradley, illustrated by Giulio Maestro, published by HarperTrophy, 1985.*

Auroras are most visible in the polar regions, so the closer you live to the Arctic or Antarctic Circles, the greater your chance of viewing them. Read the story of a boy who lives in the woods near Quebec, Canada in THE FIDDLER OF THE NORTHERN LIGHTS *by Natalie Kinsey-Warnock, illustrated by Leslie W. Bowman, published by Cobblehill, 1996. Understand the phenomenon with* NORTHERN LIGHTS *by D.M. Souza, published by First Ave. Ed., 1994.*

Icebergs are pieces of ice that break off polar ice sheets or glaciers. See DANGER—ICEBERGS! *by Roma Gans, illustrated by Richard Rosenblum, published by Thomas Crowell, 1987.*

Summers in the polar regions are wonderful! Animals get to the poles any way they can—by swimming, flying or walking. Round-the-clock sunlight promotes an abundance of food on land and in the sea.

Water Migration—Some whales don't eat during the winter. They wait until the polar summer, and then they feast! See THE WHALES *written and illustrated by Cynthia Rylant, published by Scholastic, 1996.*

Land Migration—Animals walk thousands of miles following long-traveled trails to their northern summer homes. Follow them in A CARIBOU JOURNEY *by Debbie S. Miller, illustrated by Jon Van Zyle, published by Little, Brown and Co., 1994. Do land animals migrate south to Antarctica?*

Air Migration—Birds return to the poles every year even though their flights are exhausting. Follow the migration in FLIGHT OF THE GOLDEN PLOVER *by Debbie S. Miller, illustrated by Daniel Van Zyle, published by Alaska Northwest, 1996.*

Their parents teach them! Birds, ducks and geese watch for landmarks and navigate along a familiar route. Some birds, however, migrate with no prior instruction! Read about young birds who, scientists believe, use the sun, stars and the earth's magnetic field as their guides in THIS WAY HOME *written by Lisa Westberg Peters, illustrated by Normand Chartier, published by Henry Holt, 1994.*

Blubber is fat that helps keep animals warm. Perfectly suited for icy weather with a thick layer of blubber and dense fur, polar animals have no need to head to a warmer climate in the winter. Experience the winter life of year-round polar residents in HERE IS THE ARCTIC WINTER *by Madeleine Dunphy, illustrated by Alan James Robinson, published by Hyperion, 1993.*

The native people of the Arctic include the Inuit in North America, the Saami in Europe and the Chukchi (among others) in Asia. Learn about these ancient cultures in INUIT: GLIMPSES OF AN ARCTIC PAST *by David Morrison and George-Hébert Germain, published by the Canadian Museum of Civilization, 1995.*

The Arctic

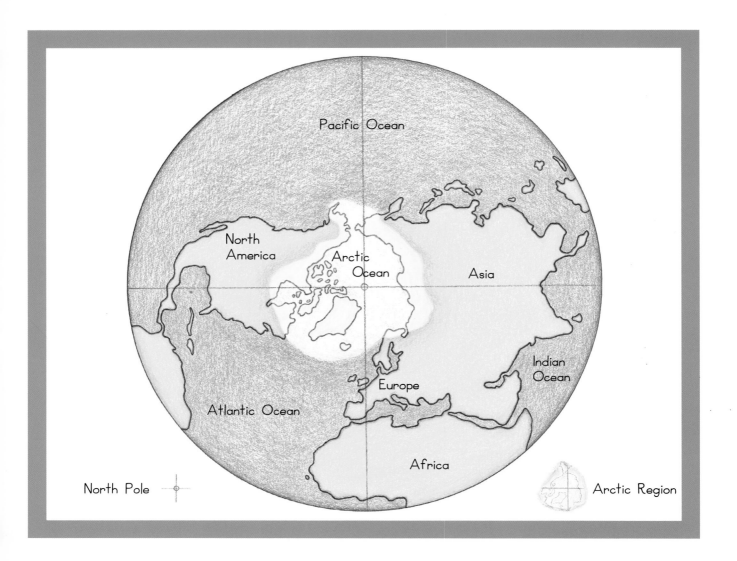

The Arctic Ocean is icy.
Continents surround the ocean.
Snow covers the land in winter.
Forests border the Arctic land.

Does the Arctic Ocean stay frozen all year?

The Arctic

Teaching Tip on page 64
Question answered on page 48

Northern Hemisphere

1.

2.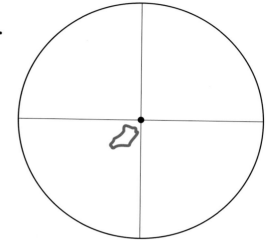

3.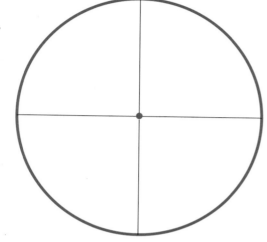

4.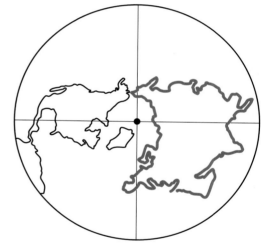

5.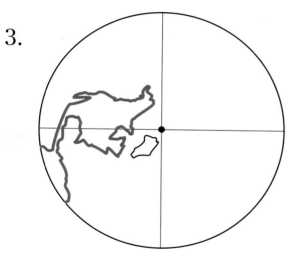

6.

Polar Bear

Question answered on page 48

1.

2.

3.

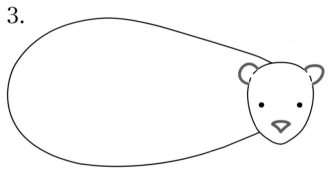

4.

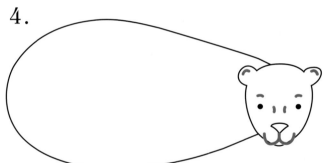

5.

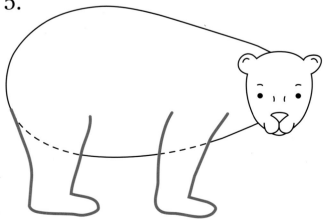

6.

Polar bears live in the Arctic.
Thick fur keeps them warm.
They are strong swimmers.
They swim in the icy ocean.

Why do Arctic foxes follow polar bears?

Walruses live in Arctic waters.
They swim under the ice.
They like to lie in the sunshine.
They rest on the drifting ice.

What are tusks?

Walrus

Question answered on page 48

1.

2.

3.

4.

5.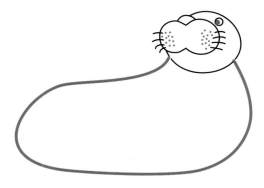

6.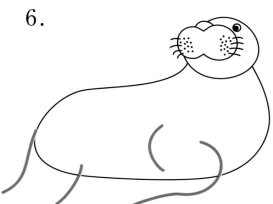

7.

8.

Arctic People

Question answered on page 48

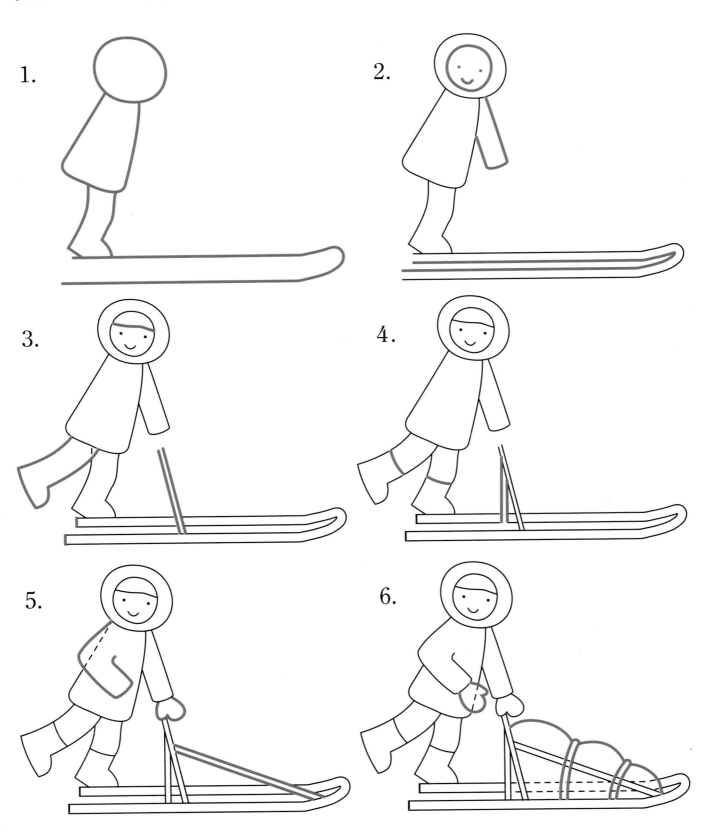

1.

2.

3.

4.

5.

6.

People live in the Arctic.
They work and play there.
Arctic winters are very cold.
People dress in warm clothes.

Arctic people build warm homes.
Most live in modern houses.
Once, many people built igloos.
Igloos are shelters made of snow.

Can people
live in
igloos all year?

Question answered on page 48

Igloo

1.

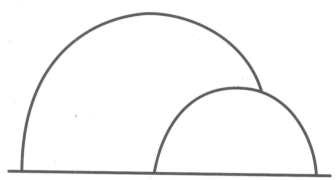

2.

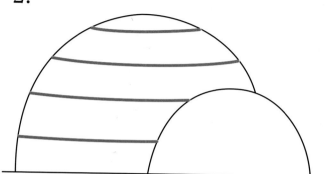

3.

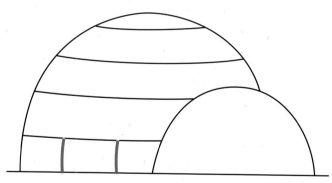

4.

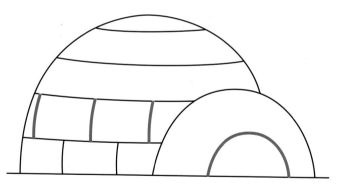

5.

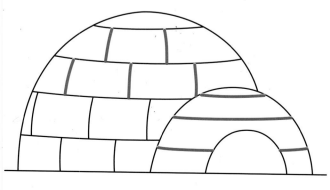

6.

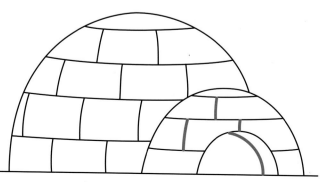

The Arctic Tundra

Question answered on page 48

Arctic Poppy

1.

2.

3.

4.
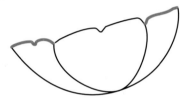

5.

6.

7.

8.

The tundra is frozen in winter.
It comes alive in summer.
The snow and ice melt.
Plants bloom and insects hatch.

What is
"The Land
of the
Midnight Sun"?

Musk oxen stay on the tundra.
They live together in herds.
They form a circle for safety.
The babies get in the center.

Do musk oxen
get hot
in summer?

Musk Ox

Teaching Tip on page 64
Question answered on page 48

1.

2.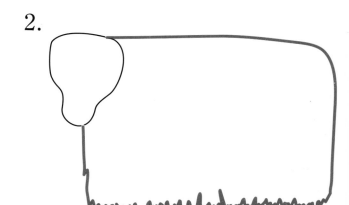

3.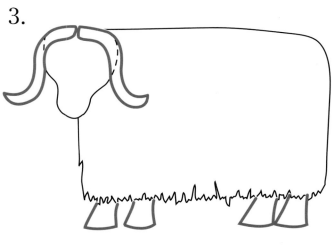

4.

5.

6.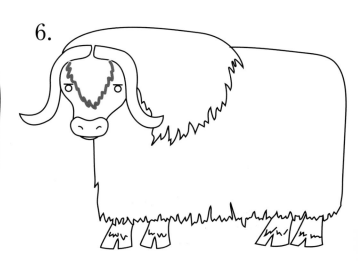

Wolf

Teaching Tip on Page 64
Question answered on page 48

1.

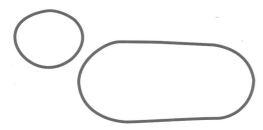

2.

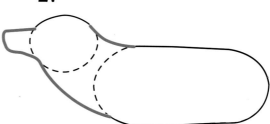

3.

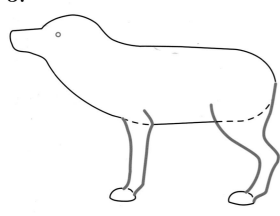

4.

5.

6.

Wolves live in the Arctic.
Some live near the forests.
Others live farther north.
The northern wolves are white.

Why are the northern wolves white?

Reindeer live in Asia and Europe.
They migrate to the tundra.
Reindeer live in herds.
Some people tame them.

Are caribou and reindeer related?

Reindeer

Teaching Tip on page 64
Question answered on page 48

1.

2.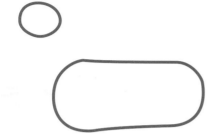

3.

4.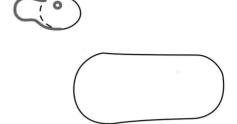

5.

6.

Draw Your World

Outlining can change the look of your drawing.

This side is outlined.

This side is not outlined.

outlined
and
colored

colored
but not
outlined

pencil

More coloring tips...

Seas, lakes and ponds
are like mirrors.
They reflect the
color of the sky.

grey sky, grey water

blue sky, blue water

(see pages 13, 22, 31 and 32)

White appears
brighter when
a little blue
is added.

white with grey added

white with blue added

(see pages 21, 31 and 36)

Hills appear rounder
when a darker
color is added along
the edge.

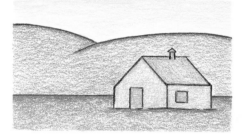

hill

hill with shaded edge

(see pages 10, 35, 44 and 57)

The location of the
sun affects the
color of the sky.

sunset

sunrise

(see pages 18, 21 and 53)

Learn more about the Arctic...

The Antarctic

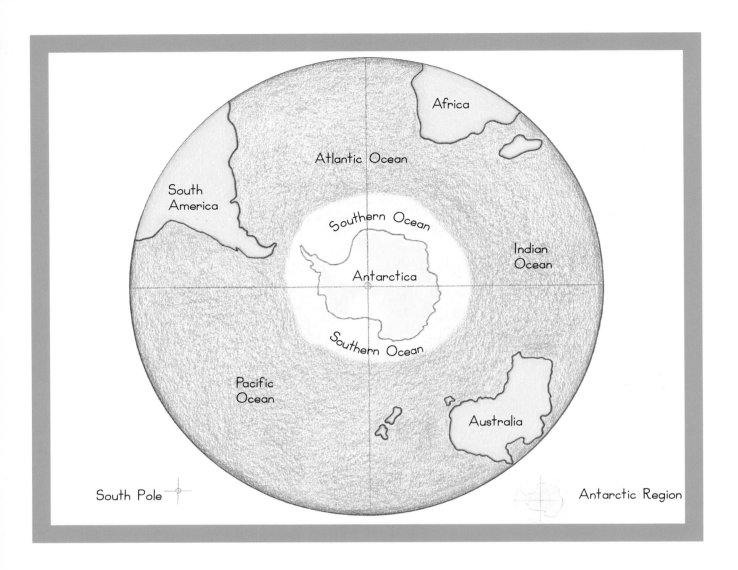

Antarctica is a continent.
It is surrounded by an ocean.
The ocean freezes in winter.
The sea ice melts in summer.

Does the ice melt on Antarctica?

The Antarctic

Teaching Tip on page 64
Question answered on page 62

Southern Hemisphere

1.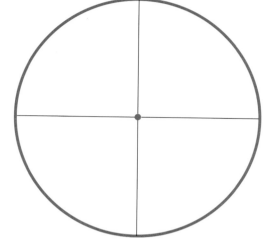

2.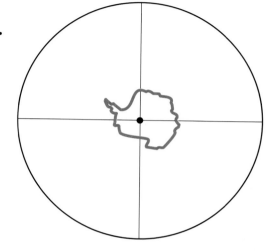

3.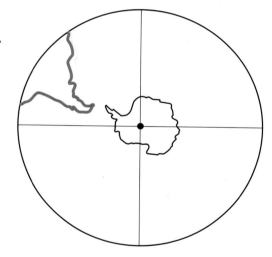

4.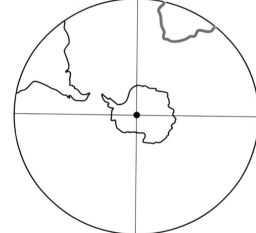

5.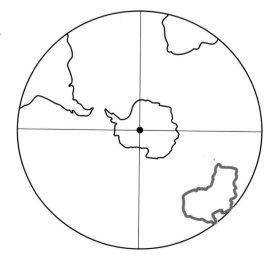

6.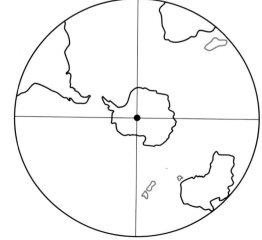

Emperor Penguin

Teaching Tip on page 64
Question answered on page 62

1.

2.

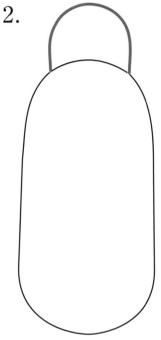

3.

4.

5.

6.

Emperor penguins are birds.

They are four feet tall.

They swim but do not fly.

They live along the coasts.

What do penguins use to build their nests?

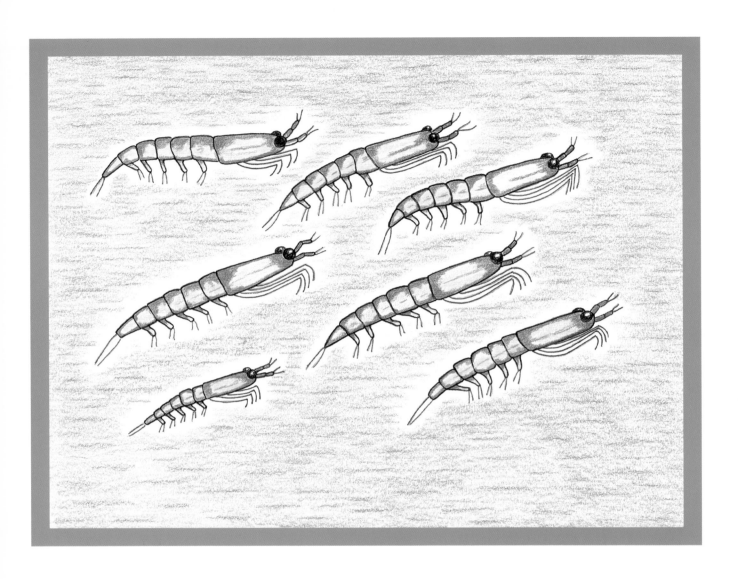

Krill are small shellfish.

Many live in the Southern Ocean.

Billions hatch each summer.

Whales and seals eat them.

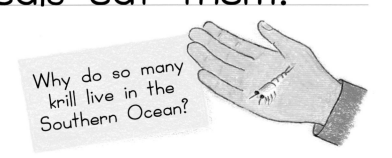

Why do so many krill live in the Southern Ocean?

Krill

Question answered on page 62

1.

2.

3.

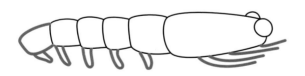

4.

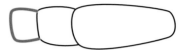

5.

6.

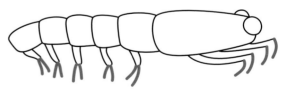

7.

8.

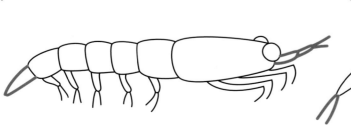

Icebreaker

Teaching Tip on page 64
Question answered on page 62

1.

2.

3.

4.

5.

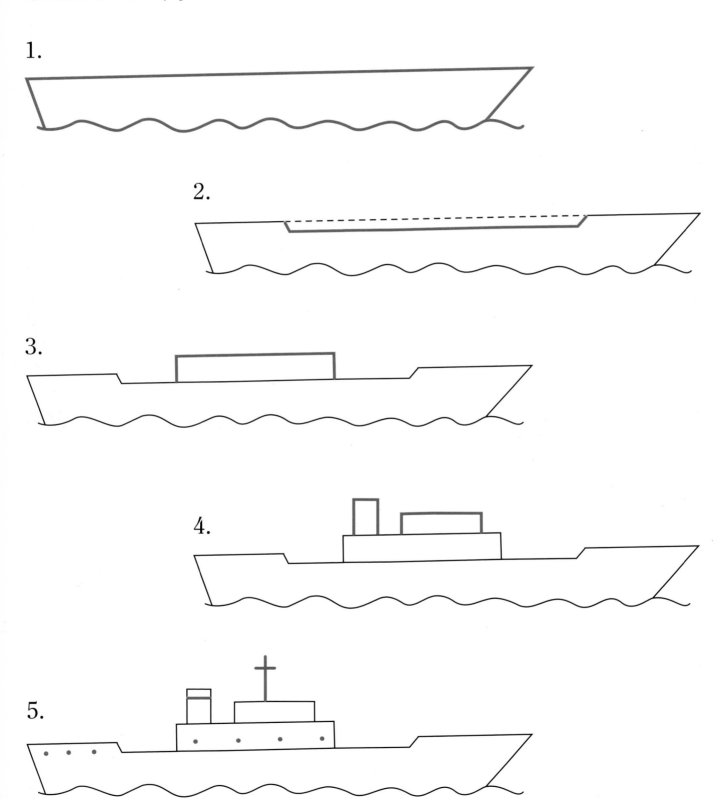

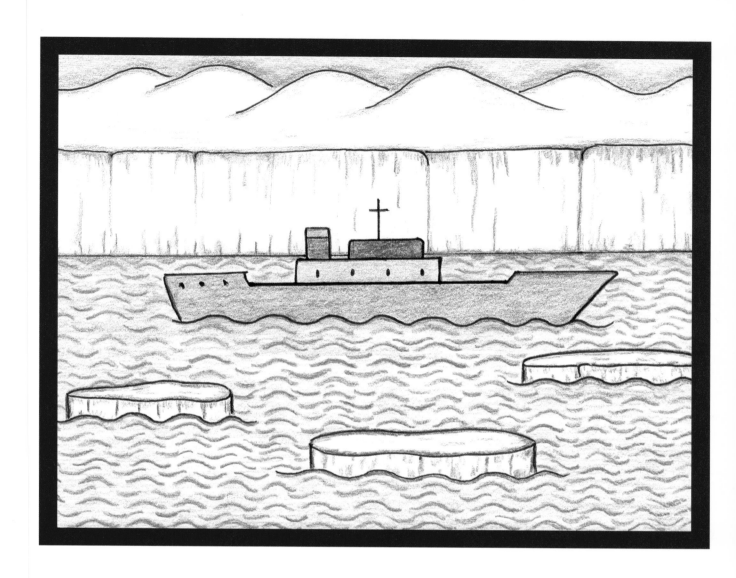

Special ships sail to Antarctica.
They are called icebreakers.
The ships push into the ice.
They break the ice into pieces.

Do other kinds of ships sail to Antarctica?

Scientists come to Antarctica.
They study geology and climate.
Some scientists study the ice.
They also study the wildlife.

How long do scientists stay in Antarctica?

Question answered on page 62

1.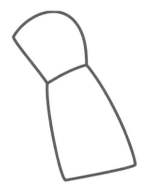

2.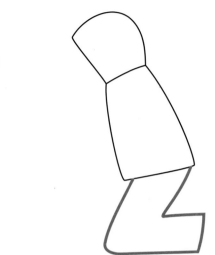

3.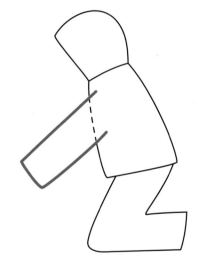

4.

5.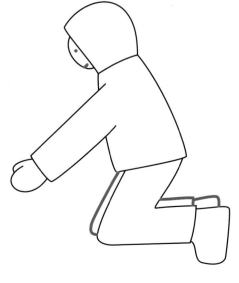

6.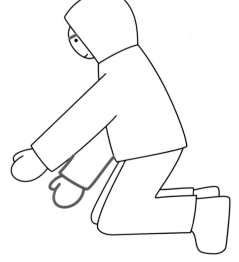

Draw From Your Imagination

Pretend you are in the Antarctic...

...playing
with penguins

...looking out the
window of an
undersea vessel

...doing research!

Imagine the colors of the Antarctic.

the Southern Lights

summer
   sunshine

slippery ice

deep,
  dark oceans

clean
water

beautiful skies

Learn more about the Antarctic...

Does the Ice Melt on Antarctica?
Page 50

Most of Antarctica is covered by massive ice fields, too thick to melt away. Some of the land is exposed during the year, but the Antarctic Peninsula, which reaches north toward South America, is the only place on the mainland where small land plants sprout. See this icy land in A FOR ANTARCTICA written and photographed by Jonathan Chester, published by Tricycle, 1995. See also EYEWITNESS BOOKS: ARCTIC & ANTARCTIC by Barbara Taylor, photographed by Geoff Brightling, published by Knopf/Dorling Kindersley, 1995.

What do Penguins Use to Build Their Nests?
Page 53

Antarctica has almost no vegetation. Instead of building a nest, the Emperor Penguin balances his mate's egg on top of his feet for two months during the winter season! About the time the egg hatches, the mother Emperor returns from hunting and swimming in the sea and helps care for their chick. Another penguin, the Adélie, uses stones to build nests. Read ANTARCTICA written and illustrated by Helen Cowcher, published by Farrar, Straus and Giroux, 1990.

There are eighteen species of penguins, but only four—the Emperor, Adélie, Southern Gentoo and Chinstrap—live on the continent of Antarctica. Study them in PENGUINS AT HOME: GENTOOS OF ANTARCTICA written and photographed by Bruce McMillan, published by Houghton Mifflin, 1993. King, Macaroni, Rockhopper and Royal penguins live farther north on small Antarctic islands.

Why do So Many Krill Live in the Southern Ocean?
Page 54

There are more minerals and nutrients in the ocean surrounding Antarctica than in any other ocean in the world. These nutrients, combined with 24 hours of sunlight, produce an abundance of plankton—primary food for krill. More plankton means more krill. More krill means more penguins, seals and whales. Understand the importance of plankton and krill with SUMMER ICE: LIFE ALONG THE ANTARCTIC PENINSULA written and photographed by Bruce McMillan, published by Houghton Mifflin, 1995.

Do Other Kinds of Ships Sail to Antarctica?
Page 57

Yes! Hunters lured into Antarctic waters by the large number of seals came in wooden sailing ships in 1820. Whale hunters soon followed. Learn about the history of the whaling industry in THE BLUE WHALE by Melissa Kim, illustrated by Shirley Felts, published by Ideal's Children's Books, 1993. A treaty signed in 1994—the Southern Ocean Whaling Sanctuary—protects all whales in the Southern Ocean.

Scientists come to Antarctica today mostly via icebreakers. Twelve countries signed a treaty in 1959 opening the continent to scientists, banning all military bases and declaring that no country owns Antarctica. In the winter of 1996, 18 countries operated 44 scientific research stations on the continent. Learn about the scientists' work from a tourist who recently visited this fascinating place in PLAYING WITH PENGUINS written and photographed by Ann McGovern, published by Scholastic, 1994.

Explorers and tourists also travel to Antarctica. They come by icebreakers, reinforced ships and even small yachts. Read about an 89-year-old explorer who recently returned to the Antarctic in ADVENTURE AT THE BOTTOM OF THE WORLD by Shelley Gill, photographed by Gordon Wiltsie, published by Paws IV, 1996.

How Long do Scientists Stay in Antarctica?
Page 58

Forty years ago, most scientists only visited Antarctica during the summer months. Now countries maintain year-round research bases, and a scientist may stay for several years. Learn about Antarctic research from the tourist's guidebook, ANTARCTICA by Jeff Rubin, published by Lonely Planet, 1996.

Adélie

Gentoo

Chinstrap

Macaroni

King

Teaching Tips

The Polar Regions

AURORAS (page 12) — People who see auroras describe them in different ways. Some people describe them as "curtains hanging in the sky." Some say they are "ribbons streaming across the sky." Others call them "lights dancing in the night sky." Photographs of the earth taken from space show tall halos encircling the top and bottom of the world. Show the children photographs of auroras and ask them to describe what they see in their own words. Encourage them to draw what they have described.

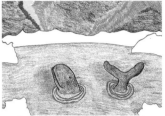

by Maggie Baker, age 9

The Arctic

THE ARCTIC (page 29) — The Arctic includes the Arctic Ocean and parts of North America, Europe and Asia. Point out that the North Pole is in the center of the Arctic Ocean. Explain to the children that, while most of the Arctic Ocean is permanently covered by a thick layer of ice, the region is arid—only about ten inches of snow fall annually. Expand your discussion to include the magnetic North Pole, the Arctic Circle, the tree line that borders the tundra and the range of the winter sea ice. As the children draw the continents, don't expect them to draw every detail. You may want to predraw the outer circle and guidelines (step 1) for the children.

WOLF (page 42) — Help the children visually estimate the length of the wolf's legs. After drawing the head and body (steps 1 and 2), look at the finished drawing (page 43) and compare the length of the legs to the width of the body. Have the children draw the feet (step 2), then ask them to consider the placement. Will the legs be the correct length? If not, have them move the feet. Once they are happy with the placement of the feet, have them add the legs (step 3).

REINDEER (page 45) — Help the children visually estimate the length of the reindeer's legs as you did in the wolf lesson. After drawing the head and body (steps 1 and 2), look at the finished drawing (page 44) and compare the length of the legs to the width of the body. Have the children draw the hooves (step 3), then ask them to consider the placement. Again, will the legs be the correct length? Are the hooves too far forward or too far back? Once they are happy with the placement of the hooves, have them add the legs (step 4).

The Antarctic

THE ANTARCTIC (page 51) — The Antarctic includes the continent of Antarctica and the ocean surrounding it—commonly called the Southern Ocean or the Antarctic Ocean. Point out that the South Pole is in the center of Antarctica (step 2). Explain that, while a thick layer of snow and ice permanently covers 98% of Antarctica, the continent is arid. Expand discussion to include the Ross and Weddell ice shelves, the Antarctic Circle and the range of the winter sea ice. As the children draw the continents, don't expect them to draw every detail. You may want to pre-draw the outer circle and guidelines (step 1) for the children.

EMPEROR PENGUIN (page 52) — Emperor Penguins are huge birds that stand up to four feet tall. Try drawing lifesize Emperors. If you have children that are close to four feet tall, have them serve as penguin-sized models. Ask the children to imagine these swift-swimming birds as they leap out of the ocean—up to seven feet in the air—and land upright on the ice.